WORKS OF GIBRAN IN THIS SERIES:

KAHLIL GIBRAN
A Self-Portrait

Kahlil Gibran

A SELF-PORTRAIT

Translated
from the Arabic
& edited by

Anthony R. Ferris

THE CITADEL PRESS
NEW YORK

THIRD PAPERBOUND EDITION, AUGUST 1969

Distributed to the Trade by
BOOK SALES, INC.
352 Park Avenue South
New York 10, N.Y.

The translator wishes to thank his brother Abdou R. Zeinoun for his personal advice and suggestions in the preparation of the manuscript for publication.

CONTENTS

CONTENTS

PREFACE

PREFACE

Kahlil Gibran (1883-1931), known to the world as the Immortal Prophet of Lebanon and the Savant of His Age, was born in the famous town of Bsharré, which prides itself on being the guardian of the forest of the Holy Cedars of Lebanon from whose lumber King Solomon built his temple in Jerusalem. His parents were Kahlil Gibran and Camila, the daughter of Father Estephan Rahmé, a Maronite Catholic priest.

When Gibran was born his parents baptized him in the Maronite Church and named him after his paternal grandfather, Gibran, according to the Lebanese custom at that time. So Gibran became known as Gibran Khalil Gibran, the name which he signed in Arabic, although in English he used the name of Kahlil Gibran.

He received his early education in his native town beginning with the study of Arabic and Syriac. Then at the age of twelve, accompanied by his mother, brother Peter, and his two sisters, Miriana and Sultana, he came to the United States and settled in the City of Boston in June, 1895.

While in Boston he attended a public school for

boys for two and a half years, after which he switched to a night school where he took general courses for a period of one year. At his insistence, his mother sent him back to Lebanon to enter the famous Madrasat Al-Hikmat, "The School of Wisdom," founded by the Savant Maronite Bishop Joseph Debs in the City of Beirut. After receiving his baccalaureate he travelled all over Syria and Lebanon visiting the historical places, ruins, and relics of the old civilization.

In 1902 he left Lebanon, never to return, for the United States, to dedicate himself to the art of painting, a hobby which he had acquired as a child.

Gibran was rather timid and unsociable; he shunned the company of his friends and neighbors in order to be left alone to devote himself to reading and meditation. As a boy, he spent most of his time reading, writing or drawing. If the other children succeeded in engaging him in conversation, he would tell them strange things which they could not understand and led them to believe that he was an odd child.

In 1908 he entered the Academy of Fine Arts in Paris where he spent three years studying under the supervision and guidance of the famous sculptor Auguste Rodin. The great man predicted a brilliant future for Gibran. Gibran's genius also inspired his friend Henri de Boufort to say, "The world must expect a lot of this Lebanese poet-artist who is today the William Blake of the twentieth century."

Upon the completion of his studies in Paris, Gibran returned to New York to stay, but each year he went to Boston, his refuge, to spend his vacation with his sister Miriana and, at the same time, to write and paint leisurely.

The note of sorrow that appears so frequently in the poems, stories, and letters of Kahlil Gibran can be traced to the frequent misfortunes that befell him in his youth. In April, 1902, his sister Sultana died; in February, 1903, his brother Peter passed away while in the spring of life; and three months later he lost his mother whom he loved to the point of veneration.

"The most beautiful word on the lips of mankind," said Gibran "is the word 'Mother,' and the most beautiful call is the call of 'my mother.' It is a word full of hope and love, a sweet and kind word coming from the depths of the heart. The mother is everything—she is our consolation in sorrow, our hope in misery, and our strength in weakness. She is the source of love, mercy, sympathy, and forgiveness. He who loses his mother loses a pure soul who blesses and guards him constantly.

"Everything in nature bespeaks the mother. The sun is the mother of earth and gives it its nourishment of heat; it never leaves the universe at night until it has put the earth to sleep to the song of the sea and the hymn of birds and brooks. And this earth is the mother of trees and flowers. It produces them, nurses them, and weans them. The trees and flowers become mothers of their great fruits and seeds. And the mother, the prototype of all existence, is the eternal spirit, full of beauty and love."

As has been observed in his many published works, widely read in several languages, the early promise Gibran showed was sustained throughout his life. In the Arabic letters which I have gathered together and translated for this book, the reader will become reaquainted with the rich symbolism which marks Gibran's unique style. Moreover, Gibran enthusiasts will be rewarded with insights that can only come through an examination of real-life relationships. Many of Gibran's closest ones can be explored through these letters. As do his poetical and philosophical works, these letters reveal the curious blending of Oriental and Occidental philosophy characteristic of Gibran's thought—a combination occasionally disconcerting to the Western mind. Sometimes one has the feeling that the emotions expressed were almost too deep for words, which seem to be wrenched from him reluctantly at the agency of some compulsive force within him.

Recent world developments have heightened interest in Arabic literature and English-speaking peoples today are making deep, exploratory studies of these venerable writings, as yet unspoiled by Western influence.

The Arabs, despite centuries of internal political turbulence and external interference, have retained and refined their strong individuality. While the Western world has been seeking practical solutions to its problems through science, the various peoples comprising the Arabic-speaking world have preferred to look at life in poetic and philosophical terms. In a cultural climate dominated by the doctrines of Mohammed and his followers, Arab writers have captured the spirit of their people, portraying their devotion to the home, and their blind fidelity to their rulers, right or wrong. Not having been exposed to religious bias or disillusioned by scientific theories, Arabic writers have felt a freedom of expression which the Western literati may well envy. They set their own unconventional pattern, and no amount of outside pressure or criticism has been able to divert them from it. In the present climate of interest in Arabic writings, no author of the East offers greater rewards than Kahlil Gibran, for he stands alone on the summit of all that is fine in Oriental literature.

It is the translator's sincerest hope that those who have read Gibran and enjoyed his works will add to their enjoyment through the perusal of this book which is a portrait of Kahlil Gibran as revealed in his letters.

ANTHONY R. FERRIS

Austin, Texas,
May 13, 1959

opposite: Facsimile of a letter from Gibran to May Ziadeh, as it appeared in the Arabic edition. For the translation, see bottom of page 84.

من جبران الى مي زياده

عزيزتي مي

انا مديون بكل ما هو « انا » الى المرأة منذ كنت طفلاً
حتى الساعة . والمرأة تفتح النوافذ في بصري والابواب في روحي.
ولولا المرأة الام ، والمرأة الشقيقة ، والمرأة الصديقة لبقيت
هاجعاً مع هؤلاء النائمين الذين ينشدون سكينة العالم بغطيطهم .

... لقد وجدت في المرض لذة نفسية تختلف بتأثيرها عن
كل لذة اخرى ، بل وجدت نوعاً من الطمأنينة يكاد يحبب اليّ
الاعتلال . ان المريض لفي مأمن من منازع واغراض الناس
والوعود والمواعيد والمخالطة والمنازعة والكلام الكثير ورنين
جرس التلفون... وقد اكتشفت شيئاً آخر اهم ، مما لا يقاس ،
من اللذة والطمأنينــة ، وهو هذا : اني في اعتلالي ادنى الى
الكليات المجردة مني اليها في صحتي . فاذا ما اسندت رأسي الى
هذه المساند واغمضت عيني عن هذا المحيط وجدتني سابحاً كالطير
فوق اودية وغابات هادئة متشحة بنقاب لطيف ووجدتني قريباً
ممن احبهم اناجيهم واحدثهم ، ولكن بدون غضب ، واشعر
شعورهم وافتكر افكارهم . يلوموني ولا يسخطون عليّ ، بل

٩٩

KAHLIL GIBRAN
A Self-Portrait

Gibran wrote this letter to his father in Bsharré to reassure him of the health of his two sisters, Miriana and Sultana. One of their relatives in the United States had written to Gibran's father and told him that both of his daughters were ill and the old man conveyed his worry to his son. Gibran's father had not noticed the date of the letter: April first, or April Fool's Day.

⫷ GIBRAN TO HIS FATHER ⫸

Beirut,
April, 1904

Dear Father:

I received your letter in which you express to me your anxiety over "sad and unexpected news." I would have felt the same way had I not known the intention of the writer and the purpose of the letter. They (may God forgive them) tell you in the letter that one of my sisters is critically ill, and again they say that the illness will involve a great deal of expense, which will make it difficult for my sisters to send you money. I have immediately found an explanation in noting that the letter was written on the first day of April. Our aunt has been accustomed to such funny and gentle jokes. Her saying that my sister has been ill for six months is as far from the truth as we are from her. During the last seven months I have received five letters from Mr. Ray who assures me that both of my sisters, Miriana and Sultana, are in excellent health. He extols their fine characters, marking Sultana's refined manners; and speaks of the resemblance between her and me both in physique and in character.

These words came from the most honest man I have ever known; from a man who loathes April Fool jokes and dislikes any fabrication which saddens the heart of another. You may rest assured that all is well and let your mind be at ease.

I am still in Beirut, although I might be away from home for a whole month touring Syria and Palestine or Egypt and Sudan with an American family for whom I have great respect. For this reason I do not know how long my stay will last in Beirut. However, I am here for personal benefit which makes it necessary for me to remain in this country a while in order to please those who care for my future. Do not ever doubt my judgment regarding what is good for me and for the fortification and betterment of my future.

This is all I can tell you—with my affection to all my relatives and loving friends, and my respect to whoever inquires about me. May God prolong your life and protect you—

Your son,
GIBRAN

Jamil Malouf, a young Lebanese poet-writer, was a great admirer of Gibran. In this letter, Gibran reveals his concern and admiration for the young poet who had left Paris to live in São Paul, Brazil. Gibran pictures his friend Jamil as a torch from heaven illuminating the path of mankind, at the same time expressing his amazement at learning of his friend's move. He presses him for a revelation of the motive that prompted him to go to São Paul and place himself among the "living dead."

ᥳᥲ᷈ TO JAMIL MALOUF ᥲᥲᷩ

Dear Brother Jamil:

When I read your letters I feel the existence of an enchanting spirit moving in this room—a beautiful and sorrowful spirit that attracts me by its undulation and makes me see you as two persons: one hovers over humanity with enormous wings similar to the wings of the seraphim whom Saint John saw standing before the Throne by the seven lamps; the other person is chained to a huge rock like Prometheus, who, in giving man the first torch of fire, brought on himself the wrath of the gods. The first person enlivens my heart and soothes my spirit because he sways with the sun rays and the frolicsome breeze of dawn; while the second person makes my heart suffer, for he is a prisoner of the vicissitudes of time. . . .

You have always been and still are capable of causing the torch of fire to come from heaven and light the path of mankind, but tell me what law or force has brought you to São Paul and fettered your body and placed you among those who died on the day of their birth and have not yet been buried? Do the Greek gods still practice their power in these days?

I have heard that you are going to return to Paris to live there. I, too, would like to go there. Is it possible that we both could meet in the City of Arts? Will we meet in the Heart of the World and visit the Opera and the French theatre and talk about the plays of Racine, Corneille, Molière, Hugo, and Sardou? Will we meet there and walk together to where the Bastille was erected and then return to our quarters feeling the gentle spirit of Rousseau and Voltaire and write about Liberty and Tyranny and destroy every Bastille that stands in every city in the Orient? Will we go to the Louvre and stand before the paintings of Raphael, Da Vinci and Corot, and write about Beauty and Love and their influence on man's heart?

Oh, brother, I feel a gnawing hunger in my heart for the approach of the great works of art, and I have a profound longing for the eternal sayings; however, this hunger and longing come out of a great power that exists in the depth of my heart—a power that wishes to announce itself hurriedly but is unable to do so, for the time has not come, and the people who died on the day of their birth are still walking and standing as a barrier in the way of the living.

My health is, as you know, like a violin in the hands of one that does not know how to play it, for it makes him hear harsh melody. My sentiments are like an ocean with their ebb and flow; my soul is like a quail with broken wings. She suffers immensely when she sees the swarms of birds hovering in the sky, for she finds herself unable to do likewise. But like all other birds, she enjoys the silence of Night, the coming of Dawn, the rays of Sun, and the beauty of the valley. I paint and write now and then, and in the midst of my paintings and writings, I am like a small boat sailing between an ocean of an endless depth and a sky of limitless blue—strange dreams, sub-

lime desires, great hopes, broken and mended thoughts;
and between all these there is something which the people
call Despair, and which I call Inferno.

GIBRAN

In the month of May, 1903, Ameen Guraieb, editor
and owner of *Almuhager,* daily Arabic newspaper published in New York, visited the city of Boston. Among
the people who received Ameen was the young Kahlil
Gibran who captured the journalist's regard with his
kind manner and intelligence.

The following day Gibran invited Guraieb to his
home. He showed him his paintings and presented
him with an old notebook in which he had set down
his thoughts and meditations. When Ameen saw the
paintings and read the poems in the notebook he realized he had discovered a genius artist, poet, and
philosopher. Thrilled by his discovery, the journalist
offered to Gibran a position as columnist on his daily
newspaper.

Thus Ameen Guraieb extracted Kahlil Gibran from
his retreat in Boston and introduced him to his Arabic
readers. "This newspaper is very fortunate," said
Guraieb in one of his editorials, "to be able to present
to the Arabic-speaking world the first literary fruit
of a young artist whose drawings are admired by the
American public. This young man is Kahlil Gibran of
Bsharré, the famous city of the braves. We publish
this essay without comments under the caption of
Tears and Laughter, leaving it up to the readers to
judge it according to their tastes." This was the first
time that Gibran saw his name in print in a daily
Arabic newspaper.

When Gibran wrote *Spirits Rebellious,* the book
containing the story of Rose El Hanie which caused
Gibran's expulsion from Lebanon and excommunica-

tion from the Church, it was his friend Ameen Guraieb who wrote the preface for the book.

As revealed in the following letter, Gibran's appreciation and love for Ameen went very deep. He wishes his friend *bon voyage*—Ameen was preparing for a trip to Lebanon—and confides in his friend traveling plans of his own.

❧ TO AMEEN GURAIEB ❧

Boston,
Feb. 12, 1908

Dear Ameen:

Only my sister Miriana knows something about this bit of news which I am going to tell you and which will make you and your neighbors rather happy: I am going to Paris, the capital of fine arts, in the late part of the coming spring, and I shall remain there one whole year. The twelve months which I am going to spend in Paris will play an important part in my every day life, for the time which I will spend in the City of Light will be, with the help of God, the beginning of a new chapter in the story of my life. I shall join a group of great artists in that great city and work under their supervision and gain a lot from their observation and benefit myself from their constructive criticism in the field of fine arts. It matters not whether they benefit me or not, because after my return from Paris to the United States, my drawings will gain more prestige, which makes the blind-rich buy more of them, not because of their artistic beauty, but because of their being painted by an artist who has spent a full year in Paris among the great European painters

I never dreamed of this voyage before, and the thought of it never did enter into my mind, for the expense of the trip would make it impossible for a man like me to undertake such a venture. But heaven, my dear Ameen, has arranged for this trip, without my being aware of it, and opened before me the way to Paris. I shall spend one whole cycle of my life there at the expense of heaven, the source of plenty.

And now, since you have heard my story you will know that my stay in Boston is neither due to my love for this city, nor to my dislike for New York. My being here is due to the presence of a she-angel who is ushering me towards a splendid future and paving for me the path to intellectual and financial success. But it makes no difference whether I am in Boston or in Paris, *Almuhager* will remain the paradise in which my soul dwells and the stage upon which my heart dances. My trip to Paris will offer me an opportunity to write about things which I cannot find or imagine in this mechanical and commercial country whose skies are replete with clamor and noise. I shall be enlightened by the social studies which I will undertake in the capital of capitals of the world where Rousseau, Lamartine and Hugo lived; and where the people love art as much as the Americans adore the Almighty Dollar.

During your absence I shall continue to contribute to every issue of *Almuhager*. I shall pour upon its pages all the affections, hopes and ideas that my heart, soul and mind contain. I am not looking forward to receiving any compensation. All I want from you is your friendship. But if you feel like adding a material debt to the many moral debts which I owe you, you may tell your editorial staff to get behind my book *Tears and Laughter* and help me reap the harvest of the many nights I have spent on its writing. Tell them to assist me in selling the book to the Arabic readers and to the merchants in New York and other states. As you know, I cannot promote the book without the help of *Almuhager*.

Be at ease and do not occupy your mind with anything other than the joy of seeing your family and beholding the beautiful scenery of Lebanon. You have worked hard enough in the last five years and you deserve a little rest. Let not your worrying about the future interfere with your tranquility. No matter what happens, *Almuhager* will ever remain the pride of all Arabic papers. A message from you, a poem from Assad Rustum, and an article from Gibran every week will be sufficient to open the eyes of the Arab world and direct their attention to Twenty-one Washington Street.*

Your introduction to my book *Spirits Rebellious* made me happy because it was free from personal comment. Monday I sent you an article for *Almuhager*; has it arrived yet? Write me a few lines in answer to this letter. I shall write you more than one letter before you leave for Lebanon. Let nothing dampen your enthusiasm for your trip. We will be unable to meet and shake hands, but we will join each other in thoughts and spirits. Seven thousand miles are but one mile, and one thousand years are but one year in the eyes of the spirit.

Miriana sends you her regards and wishes you success. May God bless you and bring you back safe to me, and may heaven shower upon you blessings, the amount

* Address of the office and publishing house of *Almuhager*.

24

of which will equal the love and respect I have in my heart
for you.

GIBRAN

It is a custom among the people of the Near East to
call each other "brother" or "sister." Close friends
and relatives other than those actually so related are
often referred to in this manner.

This letter was written to Nakhli, Gibran's first
cousin whom he addresses as brother. Gibran and
Nakhli were inseparable companions in their early
youth. They lived, slept, played, and ate together in
their home town, Bsharré, close by the Holy Cedars
of Lebanon.

Peter, Gibran's half-brother, a good singer and
lute player, entertained Gibran and Nakhli and took
good care of them. When Nakhli left Bsharré for
Brazil in search of a livelihood, Gibran kept in close
touch with him.

In the following letter, Gibran speaks to Nakhli of
his struggles and complains of the Arabic-speaking
conservative class which was accusing him of heresy
because of their feeling that his writings were poisoning the mind of the youth. Gibran later published a
story which he called "Kahlil the Heretic."

ᑫ TO NAKHLI GIBRAN ᑐ

Boston,
March 15, 1908

Dear Brother Nakhli:

I have just received your letter which filled my
soul with joy and sadness at the same time, for it brought

back to my memory pictures of those days that passed like dreams, leaving behind phantoms that come with the daylight and go with the darkness. How did those days undo themselves, and where did those nights, in which Peter lived, go? How did those hours, which Peter filled with his sweet songs and handsomeness pass away? Those days, nights and hours have disappeared like open flowers when dawn descends from the gray sky. I know that you remember those days with pain and I have noticed the phantoms of your affections between the lines of your missive, as if they came from Brazil to restore to my heart the echo of the valleys, the mountains and the rivulets surrounding Bsharré.

Life, my dear Nakhli, is like the seasons of the year. The sorrowful Autumn comes after the joyful Summer, and the raging Winter comes behind the sad Autumn, and the beautiful Spring appears after the passing of the awful Winter. Will the Spring of our life ever return so we may be happy again with the trees, smiling with the flowers, running with the brooks, and singing with the birds like we used to do in Bsharré when Peter was still alive? Will the tempest that dispersed us ever reunite us? Will we ever go back to Bsharré and meet by Saint George Church? I do not know, but I feel that life is a sort of debt and payment. It gives us today in order to take from us tomorrow. Then it gives us again and takes from us anew until we get tired of the giving and receiving and surrender to the final sleep.

You know that Gibran, who spends most of his life writing, finds enchanting pleasure in corresponding with the people he loves most. You also know that Gibran, who was very fond of Nakhli when he was a child, will never forget the man that Nakhli has become. The things which the child loves remain in the domain of the heart until old age. The most beautiful thing in life is that our souls remain hovering over the places where we once enjoyed ourselves. I am one of those who remembers such places regardless of distance or time. I do not let one single phantom disappear with the cloud, and it is my everlasting remembrance of the past that causes my sorrow sometimes. But if I had to choose between joy and sorrow, I would not exchange the sorrows of my heart for the joys of the whole world.

And now let me drop the curtain upon the past and tell you something about my present and my future, for I know that you would like to hear something about the boy you have always loved. Listen to me, and I will read to you the first chapter of Gibran's story: I am a man of weak constitution, but my health is good because I neither think about it nor have time to worry about it. I love to smoke and drink coffee. If you were to come to see me now and enter my room, you would find me behind a screen of thick smoke mingled with the aromatic scent of Yamanite coffee.

I love to work and I do not let one moment pass without working. But the days in which I find myself dormant and my thought slothful are more bitter than quinine and more severe than the teeth of the wolf. I spend my life writing and painting, and my enjoyment in these two arts is above all other enjoyments. I feel that the fires that feed the affection within me would like to dress themselves with ink and paper, but I am not sure whether the Arabic-speaking world would remain as friendly to me as it has been in the past three years. I say this because the apparition of enmity has already appeared. The people in Syria are calling me heretic, and the intelligentsia in Egypt vilifies me, saying, "He is the enemy of just laws, of family ties, and of old traditions." Those writers are telling the truth, because I do not love man-made laws and I abhor the traditions that our ancestors left us. This hatred is the fruit of my love for the sacred and spiritual kindness which should be the source of every law upon the earth, for kindness is the shadow of God in man. I know that the principles upon which I base my writings are echoes of the spirit of the great majority of the people of the world, because the tendency toward a spiritual independence is to our life as the heart is to the body. . . . Will my teaching ever be received by the Arab world, or will it die away and disappear like a shadow?

Will Gibran ever be able to deflect the people's eyes from the skulls and thorns towards the light and the truth? Or will Gibran be like so many others who returned from this world to Eternity without leaving behind any reminders of their existence? I do not know, but I feel that there is a great power in the depth of my heart that wishes to come out, and it is going to come out some day with the help of God.

I have an important news for you. On the first day of the coming June I will be leaving for Paris to join a committee of artists, and I shall remain there a whole year after which I shall return to this country. My stay there will be filled with study and research and hard work; at the same time it will be the beginning of a new life.

Remember me when you and the family gather at the table to partake of your meals, and tell your wife and the children that a certain relative, whose name is Gibran, has a loving place in his heart for every one of you.

My sister Miriana joins me in sending her regards. When I read your letter to her, it made her so happy that she was unable to hold back her tears when I ran across certain phrases. May God bless you and give you the best of health and keep you as a dear brother to

GIBRAN

❧ TO AMEEN GURAIEB ❧

Boston
March 28, 1908

Dear Ameen:

I have just locked myself up in my room behind a screen of cigarette smoke mingled with aromatic scent of Yamanite coffee to spend one hour talking to you. I am now enjoying my coffee and my smoke as well as our conversation.

You are now in the other part of the great, but small, globe, while I am still here. You are now in beautiful and peaceful Lebanon and I am in clamorous and noisy Boston. You are in the East and I am in the West, but no matter how far away you are from me, I feel that you are closer to me than ever. Man finds the expatriation of his beloved friends difficult to bear because his pleasure comes through the five senses. But Gibran's soul has already grown beyond that to a plane of higher enjoyment which does not require the mediation of the five senses. His soul

29

sees, hears, and feels, but not through the medium of eyes, ears, and fingers. His soul roams the whole world and returns without the use of feet, cars, and ships. I see Ameen far and near and I perceive everything around him as the soul regards many other invisible and voiceless objects. The subtlest beauties in our life are unseen and unheard.

How did you find Lebanon? Is it as beautiful as your yearnings promised? Or is it an arid spot where slothfulness dwells? Is Lebanon the same glorious Mountain whose beauty was sung and praised by poets like David, Isaiah, Farhat, Lamartine, and Haddad? Or is it a chain of mountains and valleys empty of geniality, aloof from beauty, and surrounded by loneliness?

Undoubtedly you shall answer all these questions in long articles to *Almuhager* and I shall read every word. But if there is something that you do not feel can be discussed publicly, tell it to me in a personal letter so that I may share your thoughts and see the reality of Lebanon through your eyes.

I am in these days like a man observing Lent and awaiting the coming of the dawn of the feast. My planned trip to Paris causes my dreams to hover around the great achievements I hope will be mine during my year in the City of Knowledge and Arts. I told you ere your departure to Lebanon that I would spend a whole year in Paris, and now I have also decided to visit Italy after the expiration of my time in Paris. I intend to spend another year visiting Italy's great museums and ruins and cities. I shall visit Venice, Florence, Rome, and Genoa; then I will return to Naples and board a boat to the United States. It will be a wonderful journey, for it will forge a golden chain connecting Gibran's sorrowful past with his happy future.

I am sure that you will pass through Paris on your way back to the United States. In Paris we shall meet and be merry; in Paris we shall quench our soul's thirst for beautiful things created by famous artists. In Paris we shall visit the Panthéon and stop for a few minutes by the tombs of Victor Hugo, Rousseau, Chateaubriand, and Renan. In Paris we shall roam the Palace of the Louvre and look upon the paintings of Raphael, Michelangelo, and Da Vinci. In Paris we shall go to the Opera and hear songs and hymns revealed by the deity to Beethoven, Wagner, Mozart, and Rossini. . . . These names, whose pronunciation is rather difficult to an Arabic-speaking person, are names of great men who founded the civilization of Europe; these are the names of men whom the earth has swallowed, but whose deeds it could not fold or engulf. The tempest is capable of laying waste the flowers but unable to harm the seeds. This is the consolation that heaven delivers to the hearts of great men who love great deeds, and this is the light which causes us—the sons of knowledge—to walk proudly upon the path of life.

I was thrilled to receive your letter from Alexandria, Egypt, and I was proud to read in *Almuhager* about the reception you and our brother Assad Rustum met in Cairo. My heart and soul rejoice every time I hear a word from you or about you. But tell me, Ameen, did you mention my name when you met with the intelligentsia of Lebanon and Egypt? Did you speak of the third name in the Trinity who is still behind the ocean? I believe that my friend Saleem Sarkis had told you about the criticism I had received from Lutfi Al-Manfaluti concerning my

31

story about Madame Rose Hanie. It was published in *Al Muayad*. I was well pleased with the criticism because I feel that such persecution is a diet for new principles, especially when it comes from a learned man like Al-Manfaluti.

My work in these days is like a chain of many rings connected with one another. I have changed my way of living and I miss some of the joys of loneliness that embraced my soul before I dreamed about going to Paris. Yesterday I was contented with playing minor parts upon the limited stage of life, but today I have realized that such contentment is a sort of sluggishness. I used to look upon life through tears and laughter, but today I see life through golden and enchanting rays of light that impart strength to the soul and courage to the heart and motion to the body. I used to be like a bird imprisoned in a cage, contenting myself with seeds dropped down to me by the hands of Destiny. But today I feel like a free bird who sees the beauty of the fields and prairies and wishes to fly in the spacious sky, mingling its affections, its fancy and its hopes with the ether.

There is something in our life which is nobler and more supreme than fame; and this *something* is the great deed that invokes fame. I feel, within me, a hidden power that wishes to dress its nakedness with a beautiful garment of great deeds. This makes me feel that I came to this world to write my name upon the face of life with big letters. Such emotion accompanies me day and night. It is this sort of sentiment that causes me to see the future surrounded by light and encircled by rapture and triumph which I have been dreaming about since I was fifteen years of age. My dreams have just begun to be realized, and I feel that my trip to Paris is going to be the first step on a ladder that reaches to heaven. I am intending to publish my book *The Broken Wings* next summer. This book is the best one I have ever written. But the one that is going to create a great movement in the Arabic-speaking world is a book of philosophy named *Religion and Religiousness,** which I started more than a year ago, and whose place to my heart is as the center to the circle. I shall finish this book in Paris, and probably will have it published at my own expense.

When you are in a beautiful spot or among learned people, or by the side of old ruins, or on the top of a high mountain, whisper my name so that my soul will go to Lebanon and hover around you and share with you the pleasure of life and all life's meanings and secrets. Remember me when you see the sun rising from behind Mount Sunnin or Fam El Mizab. Think of me when you see the sun coming down toward its setting, spreading its red garment upon the mountains and the valleys as if shedding blood instead of tears as it bids Lebanon farewell. Recall my name when you see the shepherds sitting in the shadow of the trees and blowing their reeds and filling the silent field with soothing music as did Apollo when he was exiled to this world. Think of me when you see the damsels carrying their earthenware jars filled with water upon their shoulders. Remember me when you see the Lebanese villager plowing the earth before the face of the sun, with beads of sweat adorning his forehead while his back is bent under the heavy duty of labor. Remember me when you hear the songs and hymns that Nature has woven from the sinews of moonlight, mingled with the aromatic scent

---

* This book was never finished or published.

of the valleys, mixed with the frolicsome breeze of the Holy Cedars, and poured into the hearts of the Lebanese. Remember me when the people invite you to their festivities, for your remembrance of me will bring to you pictures of my love and longing for your person and will add spiritual overtones and deeper meaning to your words and your speeches. Love and longing, my dear Ameen, are the beginning and the end of our deeds.

Now that I have written these lines to you, I feel like a child who wants to scoop the ocean water with a sea shell and place it in a small ditch he has dug in the sand of the shore. But do you not see between these lines other lines whose secrets you should inquire? They were written with the finger of the soul and the ink of the heart upon the face of love that hangs between the earth and the stars and hovers between the East and the West.

Remember me to your father, whom I admire and respect, and give my regards to your respected mother —that dear mother who gave the Arabic-speaking world a powerful figure, and bestowed upon Lebanon a brillant torch, and enriched Gibran with a very dear and beloved brother. Kindly spread my salaam among your brothers, neighbors and admirers like the frolicsome breeze of Lebanon spreads its blossoms upon the apple trees in the month of Nisan.

Miriana greets you from behind the ocean and wishes you the best of health. My relative Melhem and his daughter Zahieh asked me to send you their regards. Everybody misses you and longs to see you, oh beloved brother of

.   GIBRAN

TO NAKHLI GIBRAN

My Beloved Brother Nakhli:

Do you recall those interesting tales we used to hear during the cold rainy days while sitting around the hearth with the snow falling outside and the wind blowing between the dwellings? Do you still remember the story about the gorgeous garden with beautiful trees bearing delicious fruits? Do you also remember the end of the story which tells how those bewitched trees turned into young men whom destiny had brought into the garden? I am sure you remember all these things even without knowing that Gibran is like those bewitched young men tied with unseen chains and ruled by invisible power.

I am, my dear, Nakhli, a bewitched tree, but Sid Aladin has not yet come from behind the Seven Seas to unshackle me and loosen the magic ties and make me free and independent.

On the 14th day of the coming month I shall leave Paris, but now I am busy arranging my work and planning for the future. I am like a spinning wheel turning day and night. God only knows how busy I am. Thus heaven directs my life, and thus destiny rotates me around a certain point from which I cannot get away.

Your letter just reached me this morning, and since then I have been thinking and thinking, but I do not know what to do. Do you believe that you can help me with your thoughts and affections? Can you look into the depth of my heart and understand the misery which God has placed in it? All I ask of you is to feel with me and have faith and believe me when I tell you that I am a prisoner of time and circumstances. I am not lamenting my luck because I prefer to be like I am, and I refuse to exchange my plight for another one because I have chosen the literary life while being aware of all the obstacles and pains surrounding it.

Just think, my dear Nakhli, and ponder upon Gibran's life, for it reveals to you a sort of struggle and strife. It is a chain of connected links of misery and distress. I can say these things to you because I am very patient and glad of the existence of hardships in my life, for I hope to overcome all these difficulties. Had it not been for the presence of calamities, work and struggle would not have existed, and life would have been cold, barren and boresome.

GIBRAN

The ties of friendship were developed between Kahlil Gibran and the Lebanese artist, Yousif Howayek while they were studying art in Paris. Gibran was Howayek's inseparable friend who accompanied him to the opera, theatres, museums, galleries and other places of interest. Howayek was a great admirer of Gibran, and as a token of his admiration for the Prophet of Lebanon he worked several months on a beautiful oil portrait of Gibran and presented it to him.

⮜ TO YOUSIF HOWAYEK ⮞

Boston, 1911

Although this city is full of friends and acquaintances, I feel as if I had been exiled into a distant

36

land where life is as cold as ice and as gray as ashes and as silent as the Sphynx.

My sister is close by me, and the loving kinfolks are around me everywhere I go, and the people visit us every day and every night, but I am not happy. My work is progressing rapidly, my thoughts are calm, and I am enjoying perfect health, but I still lack happiness. My soul is hungry and thirsty for some sort of nourishment, but I don't know where to find it. The soul is a heavenly flower that cannot live in the shade, but the thorns can live everywhere.

This is the life of the oriental people who are afflicted with the disease of fine arts. This is the life of the children of Apolon who are exiled into this foreign land, whose work is strange, whose walk is slow, and whose laughter is cry.

How are you, Yousif? Are you happy among the human ghosts you witness every day on both sides of the road?

GIBRAN

In the preface of his Arabic book *May and Gibran,* Dr. Jamil Jabre wrote: "It is difficult to imagine a man and a woman falling in love without having known or met one another except by correspondence. But artists have their own unusual way of life which they themselves can only understand. This was the case of the great Lebanese woman writer, May Ziadeh and Kahlil Gibran.

"The literary and love relationship between Kahlil Gibran and May Ziadeh was not a myth or presumption, but a proven fact which was revealed to the public through some letters published by May Ziadeh after Gibran's death."

When *The Broken Wings* made its first appearance in Arabic, Gibran presented May Ziadeh with a copy of his novel and asked her to criticize it. Complying with his request, she wrote him the following letter:

∾ FROM MAY ZIADEH ∾

Cairo, Egypt,
May 12, 1912

. . . I do not agree with you on the subject of marriage, Gibran. I respect your thoughts, and I revere your ideas, for I know that you are honest and sincere in the defense of your principles that aim at a noble purpose. I am in full accord with you on the fundamental principle that advocates the freedom of woman. The woman should be free, like the man, to choose her own spouse guided not by the advice and aid of neighbors and acquaintances, but by her own personal inclinations. After choosing her life partner, a woman must bind herself completely to the duties of that partnership upon which she has embarked. You refer to these as heavy chains fabricated by the ages. Yes, I agree with you and I say that these *are* heavy chains; but remember that these chains were made by nature who made the woman what she is today. Though man's mind has reached the point of breaking the chains of customs and traditions, it has not yet reached the point of breaking the natural chains because the law of nature is above all laws. Why can't

38

a married woman meet secretly with the man she loves? Because by thus doing she will be betraying her husband and disgracing the name she has willingly accepted, and will be lowering herself in the eyes of the society of which she is a member.

At the time of marriage the woman promises to be faithful, and spiritual faithfulness is as important as physical faithfulness. At the time of matrimony she also declares and guarantees the happiness and well-being of her husband; and when she meets secretly with another man, she is already guilty of betraying society, family and duty. You may counter with, "Duty is a vague word that is hard to define in many circumstances." In a case like this we need to know "what is a family" in order to be able to ascertain the duties of its members. The roll which the woman plays in the family is the most difficult, the most humble, and the most bitter.

I myself feel the pangs of the strings that tie the woman down—those fine silky strings are like those of a spider's web, but they are as strong as golden wires. Suppose we let Selma Karamy,* the heroine of your novel, and every woman that resembles her in affections and intelligence, meet secretly with an honest man of noble character; would not this condone any woman's selecting for herself a friend, other than her husband, to meet with secretly? This would not work, even if the purpose of their secret meeting was to pray together before the shrine of the Crucified.

MAY

* The beautiful girl of Beirut in Gibran's *The Broken Wings.*

Sarkis Effandi, one of Gibran's best friends, was considered a scholar among the intelligentsia of Lebanon. He owned a publishing house and a daily Arabic newspaper called *Lisan-Ul-Hal*. In the year 1912 the Arab League of Progress, an organization composed of many literary figures joined together for the purpose of promoting Arab unity and culture, decided to honor the great Lebanese poet Khalil Effandi Mutran, who a few years later became the poet laureate of Egypt and Syria.

Since Sarkis was the head of the committee honoring the poet, he extended an invitation to his friend Gibran in New York to join them on the honor day in Beirut. Gibran could not make the trip, but he sent to Sarkis a prose poem with instructions to read it in his behalf before the poet on the day of the event. The story, which is not published in this book, was entitled "The Poet from Baalbeck." It was a eulogy in which Gibran pictured the poet laureate of the two sister countries as a prince sitting on his golden throne and receiving wise men from the East. In the story, Gibran expressed his belief in the transmigration of souls and praises the great soul that was incarnated in the honored poet's body.

～ TO SALEEM SARKIS ～

New York,
Oct. 6, 1912

Dear Sarkis Effandi,

I am sending you a story that was revealed to me by the devilish muses to honor the poet Khalil Effandi Mutran. As you notice, the story is rather short compared with the dignity of the great prince and outstanding poet. But at the same time it is long in comparison to the ones written by other poets and writers who, of course, are

40

inclined to be brief and clever, especially when it comes to honoring poets. What shall I do when the muses inspire me to write on such a subject that needs a little expatiation?

Please accept my sincerest thanks for your invitation to join you in honoring a great poet who pours his soul as wine into the cups of the Arab League of Progress, and who burns his heart as incense before the two countries [Syria and Egypt] by strengthening the ties of friendship and love between them.

To you goes my salaam mingled with my sincerest respect and admiration.

GIBRAN

◁ TO AMEEN GURAIEB ▷

Boston,
Feb. 18, 1913

Brother Ameen:

This is the last word I say to you while you are in this country. It is a word emanating from the holy of holies of the heart, mingled with a sigh of longing and a smile of hope:

Be healthy every hour of the day, and every day of the month. Enjoy beautiful things wherever you see them, and let their memory and their echo remain in your heart until the day you return to your friends and well-wishers. Meet the admirers of *Almuhager* in Egypt, Syria, and Lebanon, and speak to them of the deeds of their immigrant brethren; unfold before them that which the long distance has folded between our hearts and their hearts; and strengthen the ties that connect our souls with their souls.

Take a walk in the morning and stand on the top of one of the mountains in Lebanon and meditate upon the sun when it is rising and pouring its golden rays upon the villages and the valleys. Let these heavenly pictures remain inscribed upon your heart so that we can share them when you come back to us. Be kind enough to convey the longing of our souls and the wishes of our hearts to the youth of Lebanon. Tell the elderly men of Syria that our thoughts, affections, and dreams never leave our hearts and souls except when they fly towards them. When your boat reaches Beirut, stand on its prow and look towards Mount Sunnin and Fam El-Mizab and greet our forefathers who are sleeping under the layers of the earth, and salute the fathers and brothers who are living above the earth. Mention our works and endeavors in private and public meetings. Tell them that we are busy sowing seeds in America so that we may some day reap the harvest in Lebanon. Do and say whatever you wish provided you are happy, for your happiness is the wish and hope of every true Lebanese in the United States of America.

Miriana shakes your hand and wishes you happiness. Remember me to the well-wishers of *Almuhager* in Egypt, Syria, and Lebanon. Perchance when my name reaches their ears it will turn into a soothing tune. Goodbye, Ameen, goodbye, O dear brother of

GIBRAN

42

Every time Gibran published a book, he sent a copy to May for criticism. When *The Cortege* or *Procession*, and *The Madman* were published, May reviewed them in *Al-Hilal*, a magazine in Egypt, and wrote Gibran a special letter in which she discussed the above books. Gibran answered her and thanked her for the criticism, praising her cleverness, her vast knowledge, and her frankness. At the same time he tried to acquit himself of being in agreement with Nietzsche and to deny some ideas he wrote on passion in *The Madman*.

⮜ TO MAY ZIADEH ⮞

Dear May,

. . . All in all the madman is not I. The passion which I sought to bring out through the lips of a personage I had created does not represent my own feelings. The language that I found expressive of the desires of this madman is different from the language that I use when I sit down to converse with a friend whom I love and respect. If you really want to discover my reality through my writings, why don't you refer to the youth in the field and the soothing tune of his flute instead of the madman and his ugly cries? You will realize that the madman is no more than a link in a long chain made of metal. I do not deny that the madman was an unpolished link of rough iron, but this does not mean that the whole chain is rough. For every soul there is a season, May. The soul's winter is not like her spring, and her summer is not like her autumn. . . .

Then Gibran went on discussing his book *Tears and Laughter* whose dialogue May had criticized and enquired of its author what prompted him to write such a childish work, to which Gibran bravely answered:

. . . Now let us discuss *Tears And Laughter* for a moment. I am not afraid to tell you that this càme out before the World War. At that time I sent you a copy and never heard from you whether you received it or not. The articles in *Tears And Laughter* were the first ones that I wrote in series and published them in *Almuhager* sixteen years ago. Nasseeb Arida (may Allah forgive him) was the one who collected these articles, to which he added two more which I wrote in Paris, and published them in one book. During my childhood and the days of my youth, before the writings of *Tears And Laughter*, I wrote enough prose and poetry to fill many volumes, but I did not, and shall not, commit the crime of having them published.

GIBRAN

As the name of Kahlil Gibran was, and still is, dear to every Lebanese heart or Arabic-speaking person, so the name of Mikhail Naimay today is dear to the hearts of the sons and daughters of Lebanon.

Naimy, who is a leading literary figure in Lebanon and the Middle East, lives in seclusion in his home town, Biskinta, near Mount Sunnin in Lebanon. While in New York, Naimy and Gibran were inseparable friends, and it was to Naimy that Gibran complained and entrusted his secrets. Even on his deathbed Gibran called for Naimy, who came to stay with him at the hospital until he breathed his last.

Born in Biskinta, Lebanon, Mikhail Naimy received his early education at a parochial school conducted by the Imperial Russian Palestine Society. In 1906 he was granted a scholarship to the Seminary of Poltava in the Ukraine, where he made an extensive study of the Russian language in which he wrote poems and treatises that were widely admired. In 1916 Naimy

44

received two degress from the University of Washington. He wrote and published in Arabic many critical articles and stories while at the University. In 1916 he decided that the Arabic literary circle in New York, with the great Arabic writers, Ameen Rihani, Kahlil Gibran, Nassib Arida, and others, was to be his field.

In World War I, he served at the front with the AEF. After his honorable discharge in 1919 he returned to his literary career. In 1932 at the height of his fame he decided to return to Lebanon.

Among the works he published are *Two Generations,* a popular play; *The Cribble,* a series of critical essays; *Stages,* dealing with inner and outer life; *Once Upon a Time,* a collection of short stories; *Food for the Godward Journey,* his famous discourses; *Eyelid Whisperings,* philosophical poems; *Encounter,* a novel; *Threshing Floor* and *Light and Darkness,* philosophical contemplations; *The Memoirs of a Pitted Face,* a self-portrait of a bizarre personality; *Vineyard by the Road,* sayings and parables; *Present-Day Idols,* an analytical essay; *The World's Voice,* thoughts and meditations of life; *The Book of Mirdad,* a book for seekers after spiritual emancipation.

In his letters Kahlil Gibran addresses Mikhail Naimy sometimes as "Dear Meesha"—a diminutive for Mikhail. The long trip that Gibran refers to in the following letter was one of his usual trips to Boston where his sister Miriana lived. He also refers to *Al-Funoon,* an Arabic magazine which Gibran started, but which did not last long.

⤚ TO MIKHAIL NAIMY ⤙

New York,
Sept. 14, 1919

Dear Mikhail:

May God's peace be upon you. I have returned from my long trip and met with our brother Nasseeb and had a long discussion with him about reviving *Al-Funoon*, and the ways and means of securing its future. I interviewed many educated and half-educated people in Boston and New York regarding this matter, but all of the talks stopped at a certain point. The point is this: Nasseeb Arida cannot take the responsibility alone. It is necessary that Mikhail Naimy return to New York and join Nasseeb in the project and put it on a working basis before the intelligentsia and the merchants of New York. By having these two men working together, the confidence of the Syrian people may be gained; for one alone cannot win. An entertainment should be given in New York, and the proceeds would go to the magazine. How can the entertainment be a success when the man who is capable of obtaining speakers and musicians is in Washington? A committee should be formed to start the work. The treasurer must be known to the Syrians in other states who will ask themselves a thousand and one questions before they answer the circular. But who else other than Mikhail Naimy is capable of forming this committee?

There are numerous things, Mikhail, that begin and end with you each time we discuss the subject of *Al-Funoon*. If you wish to revive the magazine, you should come to New York and be the trigger behind every move. Nasseeb is unable to do anything at present, and of all the admirers and well-wishers of *Al-Funoon* in New York, there is no one who is capable of taking the responsibility upon himself. It is my belief that five thousand dollars would be sufficient to guarantee the future of the magazine. However, I presume that a circular without the entertainment would not bring half of the proposed amount. In short, the success of the project depends upon your presence in New York. If your return to New York means a sacrifice on your part, that sacrifice must be considered as placing that which is dear, and offering the important upon the altar of that which is more important. To me the dearest thing in your life is the realization of your dreams, and the most important thing is the reaping of the fruit of your talents.

Write me if you will; and may God protect you for your brother

G<small>IBRAN</small>

Emil Zaidan was an outstanding scholar and well known throughout the Arabic-speaking world for his great works in the field of Arabic literature. Being a Lebanese and owner and editor of one of the best Arabic magazines in Egypt, he admired Gibran and looked upon him as a genius. He devoted many pages to him in his monthly magazine *Al-Hilal*, the Crescent. It was through this magazine and many others that Gibran won fame and became known as poet, artist, and philosopher.

In the following letter to his friend Zaidan, Gibran speaks of the circumstances that made it necessary for him to work ten hours a day despite his doctor's orders that he work no more than five. Gibran at that time was working on several projects that required many hours of daily work. He tells his friend that there is nothing more difficult than the existence of a strong spirit in a weak body.

❧ TO EMIL ZAIDAN ❧

1919

My Brother Emil:

. . . My health is better now than it used to be. Yet it is still like a violin with broken strings. What is

47

bothering me most now is that circumstances have placed me in a position that require of me ten hours of daily work while I am forbidden to spend more than four or five hours writing or painting. There is nothing more difficult than the existence of a strong spirit in a weak body. I feel—I am not modest—that I am just at the beginning of a mountain road. The twenty years which I have spent as a writer and painter were but an era of preparation and desire. Up to the present time I have not yet done anything worthy of remaining before the face of the sun. My ideas have not ripened yet, and my net is still submerged in water.

GIBRAN

In this letter Gibran mentions his two friends, Abdul-Masseh and Nasseeb Arida. The former was the owner and editor of *As-Sayeh*, an Arabic newspaper published in New York, and the latter was a famous poet and owner and editor of *Al-Akhlak*, the Character, a monthly magazine published also in New York. Both Abdul-Masseh and Nasseeb were members of Arrabitah, a literary circle limited in membership to ten or thirteen, organized in New York with Gibran as president and Mikhail Naimy as secretary. Other members of Arrabitah were Catzeflis, an intimate of Gibran and an essayist of recognized accomplishments in the field of Arabian thought and literature, Ayoub, Hawie, Rihani, Abu-Mady, Nadra, Alkazin, Bahut, Atalla. Each one of these pioneers from Syria or Lebanon made a worthy contribution to poetry and literature. Gibran was the first of eight now dead. Arrabitah brought about a real renaissance in modern

Arabic literature. Many books in Arabic have already been written about it, and many more will be written.

⚈⟋ TO MIKHAIL NAIMY ⟍⚈

Boston, 1920

My Brother Mikhail:

Peace be unto you and unto your big heart and pure soul. I would like to know how you are and where you are. Are you in the forest of your dreams or in the knolls and hills of your thoughts? Or are you on the top of that mountain where all dreams turn into one vision, and all thoughts into a single ambition? Tell me where you are, Mikhail.

As to myself, I am, between my confounded health and the will of the people, like an out-of-tune musical instrument in the hands of a giant who plays on it strange melodies devoid of harmony. God help me, Mikhail, with those Americans! May God take both of us away from them to the placid valleys of Lebanon.

I have just mailed to Abdul-Masseh a short article for publication. Examine it, brother, and if it is not fit for publishing, tell Abdul-Masseh to keep it for me in an obscure corner until I return.

This article was written between midnight and dawn, and I do not know whether it is good or not. But the basic idea in it is not strange to the subject matter we discuss during our evening gathering. Tell me, how is Nasseeb and where is he? Each time I think of you and him, I feel peaceful, calm and enchantingly tranquil, and I say to myself, "Nothing is vanity under the sun."

A thousand greetings and salaams to our brethren in the spirit of truth. May God protect you and watch over you, and keep you a dear brother to your brother

GIBRAN

When Gibran published his Arabic book *The Tempest* in 1920, Naimy came out with an article praising the author and the outstanding works included in the volume.

TO MIKHAIL NAIMY

Boston, 1920

Brother Mikhail:

I have just read your article on *The Tempest*. What shall I say to you, Mikhail?

You have put between your eyes and the pages of my book a magnifying glass which made them appear greater than they really are. This made me feel ashamed of myself. You have placed, through your article, a great responsibility upon me. Will I ever be able to live up to it? Will I be able to vindicate the basic thought in the vision you have revealed of me? It seems to me that you wrote that wonderful article while looking upon my future, and not upon my past. For my past has consisted only of threads, not woven. It has also been stones of various sizes and shapes, but not a structure. I could see you looking upon me with the eye of hope, not of criticism, which makes me regret much of my past and at the same time dream about my future with a new enthusiasm in my heart. If that was what you wanted to do for me, you have succeeded, Mikhail.

I liked the stationery for Arrabitah very much, but the motto "To God many a treasure beneath the throne, etc." should be more obvious. The printing of the names of the officers and members is necessary if we wish to create the desired result. Everyone looking at a missive from Arrabitah would wonder who the members of Arrabitah are. However, I prefer that the names be printed in the smallest Arabic type.

I am sorry, Mikhail, that I shall not return to New York before the middle of next week, for I am tied up with some important problems in this abominable city. What shall I do? You all go to Milford, and replenish your cups with the wine of the spirit and the wine of the grapes, but do not forget your loving brother who is longing to see you

GIBRAN

In the following letter Gibran speaks of the meeting he and other members of Arrabitah had at the home of Rasheed Ayoub. Plans had been made at the meeting for the publication of the *Anthology of Arrabitah*, an Arabic book containing a history of the literary organization as well as a collection of stories, articles, and poems written by its members.

Gibran refers to *Barren* and *Memoirs of a Pitted Face*. These were manuscripts of Mikhail Naimy, who

51

had asked Gibran to inquire of Nasseeb Aribda as to their whereabouts.

The word *inshallah* means "God willing."

❧ TO MIKHAIL NAIMY ❧

New York,
October 8, 1920

Dear Mikhail:

Each time I think of you traveling as a salesman in the interior for a business firm, I feel somehow hurt. Yet I know that this pain is the residue of an old philosophy. Today I believe in Life and in all that she brings upon us, and I confirm that all that the days and nights bring is good, and beautiful and useful.

We met last night at Rasheed's home, and we drank and ate and listened to songs and poetry. But our evening was not complete because you were not with us in person.

The materials for the *Anthology of Arrabitah* are all ready, if only in spirit! And they are all arranged, but only in words. When I ask for something from any of our brethren, he answers me saying, "In two days" or "At the end of this week," or "Next week." The philosophy of postponement, which is oriental, almost chokes me. And the strange thing about it, Meesha, is that some people consider coquettishness as a sign of intelligence!

I have asked Nasseeb through Abdul-Masseh to look for *Barren* and *Memoirs of a Pitted Face,* and he promised to do so, *inshallah.*

I was glad to hear that your absence will not be

prolonged. Perhaps I should not be glad. Come back to us, Meesha, when you want, and you shall find us as you want us to be.

May God watch over you and keep you for your brother

GIBRAN

❧ TO MIKHAIL NAIMY ❧

Boston,
May 24, 1920

Dear Mikhail:

May God shower your good soul and big heart with peace. Arrabitah shall hold its official meeting tomorrow (Wednesday) evening. Unfortunately I shall be far away from you. Had it not been for a lecture I am going to give Thursday night, I would return to New York for the sake of Arrabitah's love. If you consider the lecture a legal excuse, I will be grateful for your generosity and consideration; otherwise you will find me willing to pay the fine of five dollars with pleasure.

This city was called in the past the city of science and art, but today it is the city of traditions. The souls of its inhabitants are petrified; even their thoughts are old and worn-out. The strange thing about this city, Mikhail, is that the petrified is always proud and boastful, and the worn-out and old holds its chin high. Many a time I have sat and conversed with Harvard professors in whose presence I felt as if I were talking to a sheik from Al-Azhar.*

On several occasions I have talked with Bostonian ladies and heard them say things which I used to hear from the ignorant and simple old ladies in Syria. Life is all the same, Mikhail; it declares itself in the villages of Lebanon as in Boston, New York, and San Francisco.

Remember me with best wishes to my brethren and fellow workers in Arrabitah. May God keep you as a dear brother to

GIBRAN

In many places throughout his writings Gibran refers to his studio in New York as "the hermitage." In this letter he speaks of his meeting there with Nasseeb Arida and Abdul-Masseh.

➤ TO MIKHAIL NAIMY ➤

New York, 1920

My Dear Meesha:

Good morning to you, oh wondering soul between the intent of the earth and the claim of heaven. I heard your voice calling the people's attention to "your goods" in the markets and squares. I heard you shouting softly, "We sell denims, we sell muslins," and I loved the soothing tone of your voice, Meesha, and I know that the angels hear you and record your calls in the Eternal Book.

* According to historians, Al-Azhar is the oldest university in the world whose sheiks (professors) stick to old traditions.

I was happy to hear about your great success. However, I fear this success! I am afraid it is going to lead you into the heart of the business world. He who reaches that heart will find it very difficult to return to our world!

I shall meet with Nasseeb and Abdul-Masseeh at the hermitage tonight and we shall discuss the *Anthology*. Wish you were with us.

I am in these days a man with a thousand and one things to do. I am like a sick bee in a garden of flowers. The nectar is ample and the sun is beautiful upon the flowers.

Pray for me and receive God's blessing, and remain a dear brother to

GIBRAN

◆◆ TO MIKHAIL NAIMY ◆◆

New York, 1920

Dear Meesha:

We have already missed you, though you have barely said goodby. What would happen to us if you stayed away three weeks?

The *Anthology:* What of it? It is a chain whose rings are made of postponement and hesitation. Every time I mention it to Nasseeb or Abdul-Masseeh, the first will say to me, "Tomorrow," and the second will respond "You are right." But in spite of all these delays, the *Anthology* will appear at the end of the year, *Inshallah*.

Write to me when you have nothing better to

55

do. If your new poem has already been completed, send
me a copy of it. You have not given me a copy of your
poem "Oh, Cup-Bearer." May God forgive you. Be as
you wish and remain a dear brother to your brother

GIBRAN

ᦒ TO MAY ZIADEH ᦒ

Nov. 1, 1920

Dear May:

The soul, May, does not see anything in life save
that which is in the soul itself. It does not believe except
in its own private event, and when it experiences something, the outcome becomes a part of it. I experienced
something last year that I intended to keep a secret, but
I did not do so. In fact, I revealed it to a friend of mine to
whom I was accustomed to reveal my secrets because I
felt that I was in dire need of talking to someone. But do
you know what she told me? She said to me without thinking, "This is a musical song." Suppose someone had told a
mother holding her babe in her arms that she was carrying
a wooden statue, what would be the answer, and how would
that mother feel about it?

Many months had passed and the words ("a
musical song") were still ringing in my ears, but my
friend was not satisfied with what she had told me, but
kept on watching me and reprimanding me for every word
I uttered, hiding everything away from me and piercing
my hand with a nail every time I attempted to touch her.

Consequently I became desperate, but despair, May, is an ebb for every flow in the heart; it's a mute affection. For this reason I have been sitting before you recently and gazing at your face without uttering a word or without having a chance to write you, for I said in my heart, "I have no chance."

Yet in every winter's heart there is a quivering spring, and behind the veil of each night there is a smiling dawn. Now my despair has turned into hope.

GIBRAN

May asked Gibran once how he wrote and how he ate and how he spent his everyday life, etc. She also inquired about his home and office and everything he did. Gibran answered some of her questions in the letter which follows.

☙ TO MAY ZIADEH ❧

1920

. . . How sweet are your questions, and how happy I am to answer them, May. Today is a day of smoking; since this morning I have already burned one million cigarettes. Smoking to me is a pleasure and not a habit. Sometimes I go for one week without smoking one single cigarette. I said that I burned one million cigarettes. It is all your fault and you are to blame. If I were by myself in this valley, I would never return . . .

As to the suit I am wearing today, it is customary to wear two suits at the same time; one suit woven by the weaver and made by the tailor and another one made out of flesh, blood, and bones. But today I am wearing one long and wide garment spotted with ink of different colors. This garment does not differ much from the ones worn by the dervishes save that it is cleaner. When I go back to the Orient I shall not wear anything but old-fashioned Oriental clothes.

. . . As regards my office, it is still without ceiling and without walls, but the seas of sands and the seas of ether are still like they were yesterday, deep with many waves and no shores. But the boat in which I sail these seas has no masts. Do you think you can provide masts for my boat?

The book *Towards God* is still in the mist factory, and its best drawing is in *The Forerunner* of which I sent you a copy two weeks ago.

> After answering some of her questions he began to describe himself to her symbolically.

What shall I tell you about a man whom God has arrested between two women, one of whom turns his dream into awakeness, and the other his awakeness into dream? What shall I say of a man whom God has placed between two lamps? Is he melancholy or is he happy? Is he a stranger in this world? I do not know. But I would like to ask you if you wish for this man to remain a stranger whose language no one in the universe speaks. I do not know. But I ask you if you would like to talk to this man in the tongue he speaks, which you can understand better than anyone else. In this world there are many who do not understand the language of my soul. And in this world there are also many who do not understand the language of your soul. I am, May, one of those upon whom life bestowed many friends and well-wishers. But tell me: is there any one among those sincere friends to whom we can say, "Please carry our cross for us only one day"? Is there any person who knows that there is one song behind our songs that cannot be sung by voices or uttered by quivering strings? Is there anyone who sees joy in our sorrow and sorrow in our joy?

... Do you recall, May, your telling me about a journalist in Buenos Aires who wrote and asked for what every newspaperman asks for—your picture? I have thought of this newspaperman's request many times, and each time I said to myself, "I am not a journalist; therefore I shall not ask for what the newspaperman asks for. No I am not a journalist. If I were the owner or editor of a magazine or newspaper, I would frankly and simply and without abashment ask her for her picture. No, I am not a journalist; what shall I do?"

GIBRAN

As-Sayeh was the name of an Arabic newspaper owned and edited by Abdul-Masseeh who was a member of Arrabitah, the literary circle. In that year Abdul-Masseeh was preparing a special issue of *As-Sayeh* and he called on Gibran and all the members of Arrabitah to contribute, which they did.

In that same year Gibran must have written an article under the caption of "The Lost One" and sent it to his friend Emil Zaidan to have it published in his magazine, *Al-Hilal*, in Egypt. The translator of these letters has not yet succeeded in finding the article which Gibran speaks of in this letter. Gibran also refers to Salloum Mokarzel. He was at that time the owner of a publishing house in New York where he published his English magazine, *The Syrian World*.

～ TO MIKHAIL NAIMY ～

Boston,
Jan. 1, 1921

Dear Meesha:

Good morning, and a happy New Year. May the Lord burden your vines with bunches of grapes, and fill your bins with wheat, and replenish your jars with oil, honey, and wine; and may Providence place your hand upon the heart of Life in order to feel the pulse of Life's heart.

This is my first letter to you in the New Year. Were I in New York, I would ask you to spend the evening with me in the peaceful hermitage. But how far am I from New York, and how far is the hermitage from me!

How are you, and what are you writing or composing, and what are you thinking? Is the special issue of *As-Sayeh* about to come out, or is it still waiting for those machines which run fast when we wish them to slow down, and slow down when we wish them to run fast? The West is a machine and everything in it is at the mercy of the machine. Yes, Meesha, even your poem, "Do the Brambles Know," is at the mercy of Salloum Mokarzel's wheels. I was indisposed last week, and for this reason I did not write anything new. But I have reviewed my article, "The Lost One," smoothed it out, and mailed it to *Al-Hilal*.

Remember me, Meesha, with love and affection to our comrades, and may God protect you as a dear brother to

GIBRAN

ᥱᔈ TO MIKHAIL NAIMY ᔈᥱ

Boston, 1921

Brother Meesha:

After I read the last number of the Arrabitah's magazine and reviewed the previous issues, I was convinced that there is a deep abyss between us and them. We cannot go to them nor can they come to us. No matter what we endeavor to do, Mikhail, we cannot free them from the slavery of superficial literary words. Spiritual freedom comes from within and not from without. You know more about this truth than any man.

Do not endeavor to awaken those whose hearts God has put to sleep for some hidden wisdom. Do whatever you wish for them, and send them whatever you like, but do not forget that you shall place a veil of doubt and suspicion upon the face of our Arrabitah. If we have any power, this power exists in our unity and aloneness. If we must cooperate and work with other people, let our cooperation be with our equals who say what we say.

... So you are on the brink of madness. This is

61

a good bit of news, majestic in its fearfulness, fearful in its majesty and beauty. I say that madness is the first step towards unselfishness. Be mad, Meesha. Be mad and tell us what is behind the veil of "sanity." The purpose of life is to bring us closer to those secrets, and madness is the only means. Be mad, and remain a mad brother to your mad brother

GIBRAN

❧ TO MIKHAIL NAIMY ❧

Boston, 1921

Dear Meesha:

Here is a gentle missive from Emil Zaidan. Read it thoroughly and take care of it to the best of your knowledge as you have always done. The heat is killing in this city and its environs. How is it in New York, and what are you doing?

In my heart, Meesha, there are shadows and images that sway, walk, and expand like mist, but I am unable to give them the form of words. Peradventure it would be better for me to keep silent until this heart returns to what it used to be a year ago. Possibly silence is better for me, but, alas! How difficult and how bitter is silence in the heart of one who has become accustomed to talking and singing.

A thousand salaams to you and to our dear brothers. May you remain a dear brother to

GIBRAN

In this letter Gibran speaks of *Al-Barq* (The Light-
ning), which was one of the leading Arabic news-
papers in Beirut. Beshara El-Koury, the editor and
owner of *Al-Barq*, was a great admirer of Gibran,
and he devoted many columns in his paper to him.
Gibran also threatens his friend Naimy, saying that
if he (Naimy) did not mail him the snapshots which
they had taken at Cahoonzie he would file two suits
against him: one in the court of friendship and the
other in the court of El-Jazzar, a Turkish ruler
known for his despotism during his reign in Syria.

TO MIKHAIL NAIMY

Boston, 1921

Dear Mikhail:

Peace be unto you. Enclosing herewith a letter
addressed to the counsellor of Arrabitah from Beshara
El-Khoury editor of *Al-Barq*. As you notice, it is a brief
and gentle missive, and it demonstrates at the same time
a sort of pain in the soul of its author—and pain is a
good sign.

What happened to the snapshots we took at
Cahoonzie? You are hereby notified that I want a copy
of each. If I do not obtain my rights, I shall file two suits
against you—one with the court of friendship, the other
with the court of Ahmad Pasha El-Jazzar.

Remember me, Meesha, to our brethren and comrades, and may God keep you dear to your brother

GIBRAN

William Catzeflis has already been identified as one of Gibran's intimates and an essayist of recognized accomplishments in the field of Arabic thought and literature. He also was one of the members of Arrabitah.

The farewell party which Gibran refers to in this letter was given in Catzeflis' honor on the occasion of the latter's departure to Lebanon on a pleasure trip. He also refers to a special Arabic dish prepared by Nasseeb Arida consisting of meat, vegetables and spices.

TO MIKHAIL NAIMY

Boston, 1921

Dear Meesha:

A thousand salaams to your heart that neither beats, nor pities, nor palpitates, nor glitters. It seems that you are ridiculing me for that which has turned my hair white and my poetry black; and you blame me for my briefness in writing and my silence about myself; and you proceed gradually to scold me, entering through the door of blasphemy. Allah be my rescue!

As to myself, I do not see any fault in you. You are perfect with your black hair covering your temples and the top of your head, and with the abundance of your poetry and prose. It seems as if you were born just as you wished to be born when you were in the state of embryo, and that you attained your wish while in the cradle. From God we came and to God we return!

I regret to be absent while Nasseeb's *meddeh* (spread) is being prepared. But what can I do if the *meddeh* cannot be spread from one city to another? It is a shame that some people can be filled with delicious things while others are hungry even for the grace of God, unable to obtain even a mouthful of it.

I am glad that Nasseeb insisted on your writing the preface to the *Anthology of Arrabitah*. Undoubtedly you have written or shall write that which shall be "a necklace about the neck of the *Anthology* and a bracelet about its wrist." May you remain, oh brother of the Arabs, a gem in the crown of literature, and a glittering star in its sky.

My health is better than it was last week. But I must keep away from working, from thinking, and even from feeling for a period of three months in order to regain my full health. As you know, Meesha, to quit working is harder than to work; and he who is accustomed to work finds rest the severest punishment.

I have done my duty towards William Catzeflis and those who wish to honor him by giving him a farewell party. I sent a telegram to William and another one to Anton Semman in response to their invitation to attend the reception in New York.

May God keep you and your brethren and mine, and may you remain a dear brother to

GIBRAN

❧ TO MIKHAIL NAIMY ❧

Boston, 1921

My Dear Meesha:

Good morning and good evening to you, and may God fill your days with songs and your nights with dreams. I am enclosing herewith a good letter and a check, which is still better, from an adherent member of Arrabitah. Will you answer the first in your good taste and perfect literary style, and accept the second as a burned incense and oil offering. Hoping that you do so, *inshallah.*

You say in your letter that you have told George* to send me the Spanish magazine and newspaper, but George has not sent them yet. May God forgive George, and may He mend George's memory with the threads of my patience and self-control. It seems to me, brother, that George has thrown the *Republic of Chile* [name of a magazine] into the waste-basket.

The cold in Boston is terrible. Everything is frozen, even the thoughts of the people are frozen. But in spite of the cold and the severe wind I am enjoying good health. My voice (or yell) is like the thunder of a volcano! And the tramping of my feet upon the ground is like a falling meteor that makes a big hollow in the ground. As to my stomach, it is like a mill whose lower stone is a file and whose upper one is a rattler! Hoping that your yell, your tramping, and your stomach are just as you like them to be whenever and wherever you want.

Give my regards to our brethren mingled with my love, my prayers, and longing. May God keep you dear to your brother

GIBRAN

When the doctors ordered Gibran in 1921 to leave New York for Boston to stay with his sister Miriana and

* A clerk in the office of *As-Sayeh.*

66

rest at home for a while, he carried with him on his way to Boston the English manuscript of *The Prophet* which he intended to publish that same year. When he arrived in Boston he was so sick that he had to postpone the publication of *The Prophet* until 1923. In the year 1918 he had published his first work in English, *The Madman,* and in 1920 *The Forerunner.* In this letter Gibran speaks of these two books and also of *Ad-Deewan,* which must have been an Arabic magazine or newspaper.

⤳ TO MIKHAIL NAIMY ⤶

Boston, 1921

Brother Meesha:

Ever since I arrived in this city I have been going from one specialist to another, and from one exhaustive examination to a more exhaustive one. It all happened because this heart of mine has lost its meter and its rhyme. And you know, Mikhail, the meter of this heart never did conform to the meters and rhymes of other hearts. But since the accidental must follow the constant as the shadow follows the substance, it was definitely decided that this lump within my chest should be in unison with that trembling mist in the firmament—that mist which is myself—called "I."

Never mind, Meesha, whatever is destined shall be. But I feel that I shall not leave the slope of this mountain before daybreak. And dawn shall throw a veil of light and gleam on everything.

When I left New York I put nothing in my valise except the manuscript of *The Prophet* and some raiments. But my old copy-books are still in the corners of that silent room. What shall I do to please you and to please the Damascus Arrabitah? The doctors have ordered me to leave all mental work. Should I be inspired within the next two weeks, I shall take my pen and jot down the inspiration; otherwise my excuse should be accepted.

I do not know when I may return to New York. The doctors say I should not return until my health returns to me. They say I must go to the country and surrender myself to simple living free from every thought and purpose and dispute. In other words, they want me to be converted into a trifling plant. For that reason I see fit that you send the picture of Arrabitah to Damascus without me in it. Or you may send the old picture after you stain my face with ink. If it is necessary, however, that Arrabitah in New York should appear in full before the Damascus Arrabitah, how would you like for Nasseeb, or Abdul-Masseeh or you (if that were possible) to translate a piece from *The Madman* or *The Forerunner*? This may seem to be a silly suggestion. But what can I do, Mikhail, when I am in such a plight? He who is unable to sew for himself a new garment must go back and mend the old one. Do you know, brother, that this ailment has caused me to postpone indefinitely the publication of *The Prophet*? I shall read with interest your article in *Ad-Deewan*. I know it is going to be just and beautiful like everything else you have written.

Remember me to my brother workers of Arrabitah. Tell them that my love for them in the fog of night is not any less than in the plain light of the day. May God protect you and watch over you and keep you a dear brother to

GIBRAN

68

Gibran had always expressed his desire for and love of death. Although he wished at all times to attain such a goal, he was extremely affected when a dear friend of his or someone that he knew passed away. Saba, who was an intimate of Gibran and a dear friend of Naimy, was taken away by death while Gibran was in Boston suffering the pangs of a severe ailment. As soon as he heard of the death of his good friend Saba he wrote to Naimy expressing his sentiments toward his departed friend.

He also tells his friend Naimy of his dream of a hermitage, a small garden, and a spring of water on the edge of one of the Lebanese valleys. He loathed this false civilization and wished to be left alone in a solitary place like Yousif El-Fakhri, one of the characters of a story that he wrote under the name of "The Tempest." Yousif at thirty years of age withdrew himself from society and departed to live in an isolated hermitage in the vicinity of Kadeesha Valley in North Lebanon.

⤜ TO MIKHAIL NAIMY ⤏

Boston, 1922

Dear Meesha:

Saba's death affected me immensely. I know that he has reached his goal, and that he has now fortified himself against things we complain of. I also know that he has attained what I wish at all times to attain. I know all that, yet it is strange that this knowledge cannot lighten my burden of sorrow. What could be the meaning of this sorrow? Saba had hopes he wanted to fulfill. His lot of hopes and dreams was equal to the lot of each one of us. Is there something in his departure, before his hopes blossomed and his dreams became fruitful, that creates this deep sorrow in our hearts? Is not my sorrow over him truly my grief over a dream I had in my youth when that youth passed away before my dream came true? Are not sorrow and regret at bereavement really forms of human selfishness?

I must not go back to New York, Meesha. The doctor has ordered me to stay away from cities. For this reason I rented a small cottage near the sea and I shall move to it with my sister in two days. I shall remain there until this heart returns to its order, or else becomes a part of the Higher Order. However, I hope to see you before summer is over. I know not how, where, or when, but things can be arranged somehow.

Your thoughts on "repudiating" the world are exactly like mine.* For a long time I have been dreaming of a hermitage, a small garden, and a spring of water. Do you recall Yousif El-Fakhri? Do you recall his obscure thoughts and his glowing awakening? Do you remember his opinion on civilization and the civilized? I say, Meesha, that the future shall place us in a hermitage on the edge of one of the Lebanese valleys. This false civilization has tightened the strings of our spirits to the breaking point. We must leave before they break. But we must remain patient until the day of departure. We must be tolerant, Meesha.

Remember me to our brethren and tell them that I love them and long to see them, and live in thought with them.

* Naimy was living at this time in a hermitage on the edge of one of the Lebanese valleys.

May God protect you, Meesha, and watch over you, and keep you a dear brother to your brother

GIBRAN

Nasseeb has already been identified as a member of Arrabitah—poet, editor and owner of *Al-Akhlak,* (the Character) which was a monthly Arabic magazine published in New York.

～ TO MIKHAIL NAIMY ～

New York,
1922

Dear Meesha:

Good evening to you. I now bring you the glad tidings that our Nasseeb is remaining with us, in us, and of us indefinitely, and his voyage to Argentina has now become ancient history.

Arrabitah did not meet the last Wednesday of this month for two reasons: The first is that you are away, and second is the non-existence of anything that calls for a meeting. I believe that the first reason is sufficient, and is the creator of the second one.

I was glad to hear that you are coming back Thursday. You have stayed too long away from us, Meesha. In your absence our circle turns into something nebulous, misty, without form or shape.

I was not pleased with your saying, "May Izrael take Mikhail."* In my opinion Mikhail is stronger than

*May the angel of death take Mikhail.

71

Izrael. The first has authority over the second, but the second has no power over the first. There are secrets in names deeper than we imagine; and their symbols are more obvious and more important than that which we think of. Mikhail has been since the beginning more powerful and more exacting than Izrael.

Till we meet again, brother. May God keep you dear to

GIBRAN

A glimpse at the following letter will reveal that Gibran was to give two readings from his books: the first from *The Madman* and *The Forerunner*, and the second from *The Prophet*. Since this letter was written in 1922 and *The Prophet* was not published until 1923, it is obvious that the second reading was from the unpublished manuscript of *The Prophet*.

The reader will also realize that the money which the Syrians and the Lebanese in Brazil had spent on the gift (the translator does not know what kind) which they sent to the President of the United States was a waste of money. In Gibran's opinion, the money should have been sent to Arrabitah for the revival of *Al-Funoon*, the short-lived Arabic magazine which Gibran founded.

∾ TO MIKHAIL NAIMY ∾

Boston, 1922

Dear Meesha:

Do not say that the climate of Boston so agreed with me that I surrendered myself to relaxation and forgot New York and my comrades and my work and duties in

72

New York. God knows that never in my life did I spend a month more full of difficulties, disasters, problems, and sorrows than the last month. I have asked myself many times if my "djinnee" or my "follower" or my "double" has turned into a devil who opposes me and shuts doors in my face and places obstacles in my way. Since my arrival in this crooked city I have been living in a hell of worldly enigmas. Had it not been for my sister, I would have left everything and returned to my hermitage, dusting the dirt of the world off my feet.

When I received your telegram this morning I felt as if I were awakened from a terrible dream. I remembered the joyful hours we spent together talking about things spiritual and artistic. I forgot that I was in a battle and that my troops were in a critical situation. Then I remembered my past troubles and the coming ones and recalled that I was obliged to remain here to fulfill my promise and carry out my engagements. I am committed, Mikhail, to giving two readings from my books this coming week—the first from *The Madman* and *The Forerunner*, and the second one from *The Prophet*, before a "respectable" audience who likes this kind of thinking and this style of expression. But the things that have kept me in this city, and that will oblige me to remain here ten more days, have nothing to do with what I have written or read, or shall write or read. They have to do with dull and wearisome things, filling the heart with thorns and gall and grasping the soul with an iron hand as rough as a steel file.

I have not forgotten that next Wednesday is the date set for Arrabitah's meeting, but what shall I do when "the eye is far of view and the hand is short of reach?" I hope that you will meet and decide what is useful, and that you will remember me with a kind word, for I am these days in dire need of good wishes from friends, and prayers from the devout. I am in need of a sweet glance from a sincere eye.

The gift from our brethren in Brazil will reach the White House, and the President of the United States will thank them for their generosity and kind intentions. All that shall be arranged in a beautiful manner. But a wave from the sea of oblivion shall submerge the matter from beginning to end. Meanwhile, *Al-Funoon* magazine is still asleep and Arrabitah is poor, and our brethren in Brazil and the United States neither remember the first, nor feel the presence of the second. How strange people are, Meesha, and what strangers we both are among them!

GIBRAN

Emil Zaidan was editor of *Al-Hilal*, an outstanding Arabic magazine published in Egypt, to which Gibran contributed many articles.

TO EMIL ZAIDAN

In the late
part of 1922

My Brother Emil,

... I have intended to visit Egypt and Lebanon this year, but the indisposition which kept me away from work for twelve months has set me back two years and caused me to postpone those literary and technical treatises which I once talked to you about. I must now remain in this country until my English book *The Prophet* comes out. At the same time I will be finishing some paintings that I promised to complete.

I am already longing for the Orient in spite of what some friends write to me, which sometimes makes me feel discouraged and causes me to prefer expatriation and living among strangers to the exile of living among relatives. Nevertheless, I shall return to my "old home" to see with my own eyes what has become of it.

Remain a dear brother to

GIBRAN

In introducing Mikhail Naimy, the translator referred to *The Cribble,* a series of critical essays, called *Algourbal* in Arabic.

Naimy and Nasseeb had written a poem together and promised to send it to Gibran. At the same time they must have asked Rasheed and Gibran to write something for publication. Rasheed, however, kept postponing, which made Gibran feel empty-handed also.

༄ TO MIKHAIL NAIMY ༄

Boston,
August 11, 1923

Dear Brother Meesha:

Good morning to you. I was glad to learn that your book *The Cribble* is out. But I do not mind telling you that I did not like for it to come at this time of the year, although I know that the value of the book, which is unique of its kind, has nothing to do with the season or decade. Never mind, whatever is published is published.

I have spent many long hours with Archmandrite Beshir reviewing the translation of *The Madman* and *The Forerunner*. In spite of my rebellion, I was pleased with the man's enthusiasm and determination. When we finished reviewing and correcting he said to me, "I shall submit the translations of the two books to Mikhail Naimy and Nasseeb Arida and ask them to be unmerciful in their criticism." I liked his tact and I knew that he was truly seeking enlightenment.

I have not done anything worth mentioning since I left New York other than writing down some headings and renovating some old ideas. It seems to me, Meesha, that the orderly life in my sister's home pulls me away from creative writing. It is strange that chaotic living is the best sharpener for my imagination.

I shall be happy to receive your and Nasseeb's new poem, but I shall stand ashamed and empty-handed before both of you. I may not be the only one if Rasheed keeps on postponing. If he keeps this up, I do not know how he is going to have his book of poems published.

Give my salaam and love to our comrades and tell them that life without them is miserable. May God bless you, Meesha, and keep you a dear brother to your brother

GIBRAN

76

❧ TO MIKHAIL NAIMY ❧

Beloved Brother Meesha:

Forgive my long silence and help me obtain forgiveness from your brethren and mine. Early this summer the doctor told me to abstain from all kinds of writing, and I submitted to him after a great struggle between me and my will and the will of my sister and some friends. The result turned out to be good, for I am now closer to being in normal health than at any time during the last two years. My being away from the city, living a simple, quiet, and orderly life near the sea and the woods, has stilled the palpitations of my heart and altered my trembling hand to one that writes these lines.

I shall return to New York in two or three weeks and present myself to my brethren. If they take me into their midst, I shall know how affectionate they are. A beggar should not be demanding, and a criminal should make no conditions.

This is the first letter I have written to you for three months!

A thousand salaams to all, and may God protect you and keep you for your brother

GIBRAN

❧ TO MIKHAIL NAIMY ❧

Boston, 1923

I congratulate you and offer my felicitations upon *The Cribble*. Undoubtedly it is the first living breeze of that divine tempest which shall weed out all the dead wood in our literary forests. I have read the book thoroughly, from Aleph to Yey,* and I was reassured of a truth that I had long believed and which I once expressed to you. It is this: had you not been a poet and writer, you would not have reached your goal of critic, and you would not have succeeded in lifting the curtain to reveal the truth about poetry, poets, writing and writers. I say, Meesha, that had you not undertaken the task of poetry in your own heart, you could not have discovered the poetic experiences of others. And had you not taken a long walk in the garden of poetry, you would not have rebelled against those who walk only the dark and narrow paths of meters and rhymes. Sainte-Beuve, Ruskin and Walter Pater were artists before and after they criticised the artistic works of others and each one of them criticised through the help of the light of his own inner feelings, and not through the help of acquired taste. The spiritual light that comes from within is the source of everything beautiful and noble. This light turns criticism into a fine and magnificent art. Without this light, criticism is compulsive and boring and lacking the positive note of decisive persuasion.

Yes, Meesha, you are a poet and a thinker before everything else, and your unique power of criticism is the

* Aleph to Yey means A to Z.

outcome of your keen poetic thinking and feeling. Don't give the example of the "egg"*—I shall never accept it— for it smacks of empty controversy rather than demonstrable logic.

GIBRAN

In 1924, the Syrians apparently raised funds and built an orphanage, which Gibran calls "the noblest Syrian institution in the United States." He had planned to attend the dedication of the orphanage, but when the time came, he was ill in Boston with a stomach ailment.

TO MIKHAIL NAIMY

Boston,
Sept. 7, 1924

Dear Mikhail:

I have been locked in my room for several days and I have just left the bed to write you this letter. You know that I was indisposed when I left New York, and I have been fighting the poisoning in my stomach ever since. Had it not been for this, I would not have hesitated to go to the orphanage on the day of its dedication.

You realize, Meesha, that no matter how important and pressing my work is, it cannot keep me from absenting myself two or three days, especially when I am to take part in the dedication of the noblest Syrian insti-

---

* Gibran refers here to the old Arabic inquiry as to which came first—the egg or the hen.

tution in the United States. I beg you to offer my excuse
to the Archbishop and to explain to him the real reason
for my failure to come.

GIBRAN

Abdul-Masseh, owner and editor of *As-Sayeh*, had
called on Gibran to make a special design for the
annual special issue which came out in the form of a
magazine rather than a paper and contained articles,
poems, stories and pictures of the members of Arrabitah and other Arab writers.

TO MIKHAIL NAIMY

Boston, 1925

Dear Meesha:

Peace be unto your soul. As per your request, I
have just mailed you the design for the cover of the special
issue of *As-Sayeh*. The requests of princes are the princes
of requests! I beg you to urge Abdul-Masseeh to keep the
design for me after the engraver is finished with it.

I have been wondering if you have found solitude and peace in the hermitage! I was afraid that you
might find it cold; and I should have told you of the elec-
tric apparatus which can warm one of its corners. Of
course, warm hearts do not need outside heat.

I shall return to New York in a week, more or
less, and we shall have long talks of things beneath the
earth and above the clouds. May God keep you, Meesha,
a beloved brother to

GIBRAN

P.S. I shall return to New York in ten days, *inshallah,* and we shall have a long discussion and set the drawings for Rasheed's book and share many beautiful dreams.

Edmond Wehby translated "The Crucified" from the Arabic to French and published it in *La Syrie,* a daily French newspaper in Beirut. A copy of the translation was sent by the translator to the author accompanied by a nice letter to which Gibran wrote the following answer:

∽ TO EDMOND WEHBY ∾

New York,
March 12, 1925

Dear Brother:

Peace be unto you. I was very happy to receive your very kind letter. It revealed to me the abundance of your learning and the beauty of your spirit and your zeal for the arts and artists. I wish I were worthy of the praises and honor which you have accorded me in your missive, and I hope that I will be able to live up to the beautiful things you have said about me.

I have read with admiration your French translation of "The Crucified"—however, I was sorry to learn about the spiritual condition of Syrian and Lebanese youth today and their tendency towards learning foreign languages and neglecting their own tongue, which prompted your zeal to translate a piece especially written for that young generation in the language of their forefathers.

But your enthusiasm for Arrabitah and the deeds of its workers shows eagerness in your heart and willingness in your spirit for renovation, growth and enlightenment. Now in behalf of my brethren and fellow-workers of Arrabitah I offer to you thanks and gratitude.

Please accept my sincerest respect accompanied with my best wishes, and may Allah protect you and keep you.

GIBRAN

P.S. Please remember me to my great literary brother Felix Farris and give him my salaam.

TO MAY ZIADEH

1925

Dear May:

. . . What shall I say to you about my vicissitudes? A year ago I was living in peace and tranquility, but today my tranquility has turned into clamor, and my peace into strife. The people devour my days and my nights and submerge my life in their conflicts and desires. Many a time I have fled from this awful city* to a remote place to be away from the people and from the shadow of myself. The Americans are a mighty people who never give up or get tired or sleep or dream. If these people hate someone, they will kill him by negligence, and if they like or love a person, they will shower him with affection.

* New York.

He who wishes to live in New York must be a sharp sword in a sheath of honey. The sword is to repel those who are desirous of killing time, and the honey is to satisfy their hunger.

The day will come when I will be leaving for the Orient. My longing for my country almost melts my heart. Had it not been for this cage which I have woven with my own hands, I would have caught the first boat sailing towards the Orient. But what man is capable of leaving an edifice on whose construction he has spent all his life, even though that edifice is his own prison? It is difficult to get rid of it in one day ...

... So you want me to smile and forgive. I have been smiling a lot since this morning, and I am now all smiles deep down in my heart. I smile as if I were born to smile. . . . But forgiveness is a horrible word which makes me stand in fear and shame. The noble soul that humbles herself to that extent is closer to the angels than to human beings. . . . I alone am to blame, and I have done wrong in my silence and despair. For this reason I ask you to forget what I have done and to forgive me.

GIBRAN

TO MAY ZIADEH

In the year 1926

Dear May:

... You say that I am an artist and a poet. I am neither an artist, May, nor a poet. I have spent my days writing and painting, but I am not in accord with my days and my nights. I am a cloud, May—a cloud that mingles with objects, but never becomes united with them. I am a cloud, and in the cloud is my solitude, my loneliness, my hunger, and my thirst. But my calamity is that the cloud, which is my reality, longs to hear someone say, "You are not alone in this world but we are two together, and I know who you are."

... Tell me, May, is there any other person over there capable of and willing to say to me, "I am another cloud; O, cloud, let us spread ourselves over the mountains and in the valleys: let us walk between and above the trees, let us cover the high rocks, let us penetrate the heart of the human race, let us roam the unknown and the fortified distant places." Tell me, May, is there anyone who is capable of and willing to say at least one of these words?

GIBRAN

⤙ TO MAY ZIADEH ⤚

1928

Dear May:

I am indebted for all that I call "I" to women, ever since I was an infant. Women opened the windows of my eyes and the doors of my spirit. Had it not been for the woman-mother, the woman-sister, and the woman-friend, I would have been sleeping among those who seek the tranquility of the world with their snoring.

... I have found pleasure in being ill. This

pleasure differs with its effect from any other pleasure. I have found a sort of tranquility that makes me love illness. The sick man is safe from people's strife, demands, dates and appointments, excess of talking, and ringing of telephones . . . I have found another kind of enjoyment through illness which is more important and unmeasurable. I have found that I am closer to abstract things in my sickness than in health. When I lay my head upon the pillow and close my eyes and lose myself to the world, I find myself flying like a bird over serene valleys and forests, wrapped in a gentle veil. I see myself close to those whom my heart has loved, calling and talking to them, but without anger and with the same feelings they feel and the same thoughts they think. They lay their hands now and then upon my forehead to bless me.

. . . I wish I were sick in Egypt or in my country so I might be close to the ones I love.* Do you know, May, that every morning and every evening I find myself in a home in Cairo with you sitting before me reading the last article I wrote or the one you wrote which has not yet been published.

. . . Do you realize, May, that whenever I think of the Departure which the people call Death, I find pleasure in such thinking and great longing for such departure. But then I return to myself and remember that there is one word I must say before I depart. I become perplexed between my disability and my obligation and I give up hope. No, I have not said my word yet, and nothing but smoke has come out from this light. This is what makes me feel that cessation of work is more bitter than gall. I say this to you, May, and I don't say it to anyone else: If

* At the writing of this letter May was living in Cairo, Egypt.

I don't depart before I spell and pronounce my word, I will return to say the word which is now hanging like a cloud in the sky of my heart.

... Does this sound strange to you? The strangest things are the closest to the real truth. In the will of man there is a power of longing which turns the mist in ourselves into sun.

GIBRAN

This letter was written in the year 1928 when Gibran's book, *Jesus the Son of Man,* was published by Alfred A. Knopf. In this book Gibran speaks of Jesus in behalf of seventy-nine persons who saw him. The last man who speaks of Jesus in the book is a man from Lebanon who lives in the twentieth century.

As we notice in the following letter, Gibran wrote this book while he was ill.

⚭ TO MIKHAIL NAIMY ⚭

Boston, 1928

Dear Meesha:

Peace be unto your soul. How nice of you and typical of your big heart to inquire about my health. I was inflicted with a disease called summer rheumatism which departed from me with the departure of the summer and its heat.

I have learned that you returned to New Babylon* three weeks ago. Tell us, O Spring of Youth, what kind of treasures have you brought back with you as a

* New York.

result of your bodily and spiritual absence? I shall return to New York in a week, and I shall search your pockets to find out what you have brought with you.

The book of *Jesus* has taken all my summer, with me ill one day and well another. And I might as well tell you that my heart is still in it in spite of the fact that it has already been published and has flown away from this cage.

GIBRAN

The Garden of the Prophet, which Gibran speaks of in this letter, was published by Alfred A. Knopf in the year 1933, two years after Gibran's death. Gibran did not live to complete it. The book was later finished by Barbara Young, the author of *This Man from Lebanon*, a study of Kahlil Gibran.

⤳ TO MIKHAIL NAIMY ⤳

Boston,
March, 1929

Dear Meesha:

How sweet and how tender of you to ask about my health. I am at present in an "acceptable" state, Meesha. The pains of rheumatism are gone, and the swelling has turned to something opposite. But the ailment has settled in a place deeper than muscles and bones. I have always wondered if I was in a state of health or illness.

It is a plight, Meesha, to be always between health and illness. It is one of the seasons of my life; and in your life and my life there are winter and spring, and you and I cannot know truly which one is preferable to the other. When we meet again I shall tell you what happened to me, and then you shall know why I once cried out to you, saying, "You have your Lebanon, and I have mine."

There is nothing like lemon among all the fruits, and I take lemon every day. . . . I leave the rest to God!

I have told you in a previous letter that the doctors warned me against working. Yet there is nothing I can do but work, at least with my mind, or at least for spite . . . What do you think of a book composed of four stories on the lives of Michelangelo, Shakespeare, Spinoza and Beethoven? What would you say if I showed their achievements to be the unavoidable outcome of pain, ambition, "expatriation" and hope moving in the human heart? What is your opinion of a book of this kind?

So much for that. But as to the writing of *The Garden of the Prophet*, it is definitely decided, but I find it wise to get away from the publishers at present.

My salaams to our beloved brethren. May God keep you a brother to

GIBRAN

ᕲ TO MIKHAIL NAIMY ᕲ

Telegram dated
March 26, 1929

Dear Meesha:

I was deeply touched by your telegram. I am better. The return of health will be slow. That is worse than illness. All will be well with me gradually. My love to you and to all our comrades.

GIBRAN

⌘ TO MIKHAIL NAIMY ⌘

Boston,
May 22, 1929

Brother Meesha:

I feel better today than when I left New York. How great is my need for relaxation far away from the clamorous society and its problems. I shall rest and be away, but I would remain close to you and to my brethren in spirit and love. Do not forget me; keep in touch with me.

A thousand salaams to you, and Abdul-Masseeh, and to Rasheed and William and Nasseeb and to each one connected with us in Arrabitah.*

May heaven protect you and bless you, brother.

GIBRAN

⌘ TO MAY ZIADEH ⌘

1930

Dear May:

. . . I have many things to discuss with you concerning the transparent element and other elements. But

---

* Arrabitah means "bond" in Arabic, and since this is a literary society, the meaning here is "pen bond."

I must remain silent and say nothing about them until the cloud is dispersed and the doors of the ages are opened, whereupon the Angel of God will say to me: "Speak, for the days of silence are gone; walk, for you have tarried too long in the shadow of bewilderment." I wonder when will the doors open so that the cloud may be dispersed!

. . . We have already reached the summit, and the plains and the valleys and the forests have appeared before us. Let us rest, May, and talk a while. We cannot remain here long, for I see a higher peak from a distance, and we must reach it before sunset. We have already crossed the mountain road in confusion, and I confess to you that I was in a hurry and not always wise. But isn't there something in life which the hands of wisdom cannot reach? Isn't there something which petrifies wisdom? Waiting is the hoofs of time, May, and I am always awaiting that which is unknown to me. It seems sometimes that I am expecting something to happen which has not happened yet. I am like those infirms who used to sit by the lake waiting for the coming of the angel to stir the water for them. Now the angel has already stirred the water, but who is going to drop me in it? I shall walk in that awful and bewitched place with resolution in my eyes and my feet.

GIBRAN

Dear May:

 . . . My health at present is worse than it was at the beginning of the summer. The long months which I spent between the sea and the country have prolonged the distance between my body and my spirit. But this strange heart that used to quiver more than one hundred times a minute is now slowing down and is beginning to go back to normal after having ruined my health and affected my well-being. Rest will benefit me in a way, but the doctor's medicines are to my ailment as the oil to the lamp. I am in no need for the doctors and their remedies, nor for rest and silence. I am in dire need for one who will relieve me by lightening my burden. I am in need of a spiritual remedy—for a helpful hand to alleviate my congested spirit. I am in need of a strong wind that will fell my fruits and my leaves.

 . . . I am, May, a small volcano whose opening has been closed. If I were able today to write something great and beautiful, I would be completely cured. If I could cry out, I would gain back my health. You may say to me, "Why don't you write in order to be cured; and why don't you cry out in order to gain back your health?" And my answer is: I don't know. I am unable to shout, and this is my very ailment; it's a spiritual ailment whose symptoms have appeared in the body . . . You may ask again, "Then what are you doing for this ailment, and what will be the outcome, and how long are you going to remain in this plight?" And I say to you that I shall be cured, and I shall sing my song and rest later, and I shall cry out with a loud voice that will emanate from the depth of my silence. Please, for God's sake, don't tell me, "You have sung a lot, and what you have already sung was beautiful." Don't mention to me my past deeds, for the remembrance of them makes me suffer, and their triviality turns my blood into a burning fire, and their dryness generates thirst in my heart, and their weakness keeps me up and down one thousand and one times a day. Why did I write all those articles and stories? I was born to live and to write a book—only one small book—I was born to live and suffer and to say one living and winged word, and I cannot remain silent until Life utters that word through my lips. I was unable to do this because I was a prattler. It's a shame, and I am filled with regret because I remained a chatterbox until my jabbering weakened my strength. And when I became able to utter the first letter of my word, I found myself down on my back with a stone in my mouth . . . However, my word is still in my heart, and it is a living and a winged word which I must utter in order to remove with its harmony the sins which my jabbering has created.

The torch must come forth.

GIBRAN

When Felix Farris, a prominent Lebanese writer, heard about his beloved Gibran's illness, he felt so bad that he forgot about his own illness, and wrote to

Gibran the letter which follows. Gibran's answer is next included.

❧ FROM FELIX FARRIS ❧

1930

. . . Gibran, my seeing you ill was more painful to me than my own illness. Come let us go to the native land of the body and enliven it there. When the tempest of pain strikes a person, the body longs for its earth and the soul for its substance.

Come, my brother, let us discard what is broken, and fly away with the unbroken to the place where silence lives. There is a longing in my heart for you like the longing for the place in which I left my heart. There in Beirut, at the harbor, my eyes shall focus upon the heart of the Holy Cedars, the paradise of my country. With you by me, Gibran, my soul would look at its eternal Cedars as if it were on the shore of the true Universe. Let us triumph and remedy our ailments. This civilization which has tired you after many years, has exausted me many months ago. Come, let us withdraw and exploit our suffering under the shade of the Cedars and the pine trees, for there we shall be closer to the earth and nearer to heaven. . . . My eyes are anxious to see the dust of the earth and all that is within it of importance in the hidden world.

Believe me, Gibran, I have not seen a blooming flower, nor have I smelled an aromatic scent, nor heard the singing of a nightingale, nor felt the passing of a frolicsome breeze since the last time my eyes saw the Orient, your home and mine.

Come, let us awaken the dormant pains—come and let the pure skies of your country hear your beautiful songs, and let your brush and pen draw from the original what you are drawing now from the prints of memory.

Felix Farris

ꬠ TO FELIX FARRIS ꬠ

1930

My dear Felix,

. . . It is not strange that we are both struck by the same arrow at the same time. Pain, my brother, is an unseen and powerful hand that breaks the skin of the stone in order to extract the pulp. I am still at the mercy of the doctors and I shall remain subject to their weights and measures until my body rebels against them or my soul revolts against my body. Mutiny shall come in the form of surrender and surrender in the form of mutiny; but whether I rebel or not, I must go back to Lebanon, and I must withdraw myself from this civilization that runs on wheels. However, I deem it wise not to leave this country before I break the strings and chains that tie me down; and numerous are those strings and those chains! I wish to go back to Lebanon and remain there forever.

Gibran